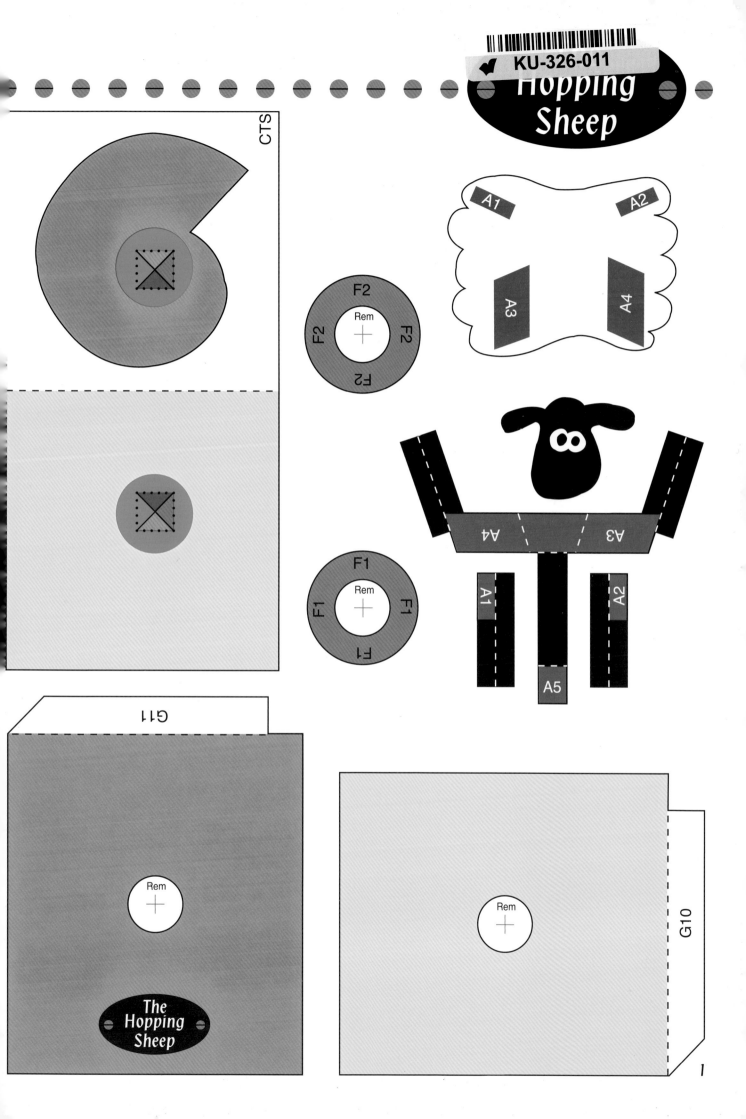

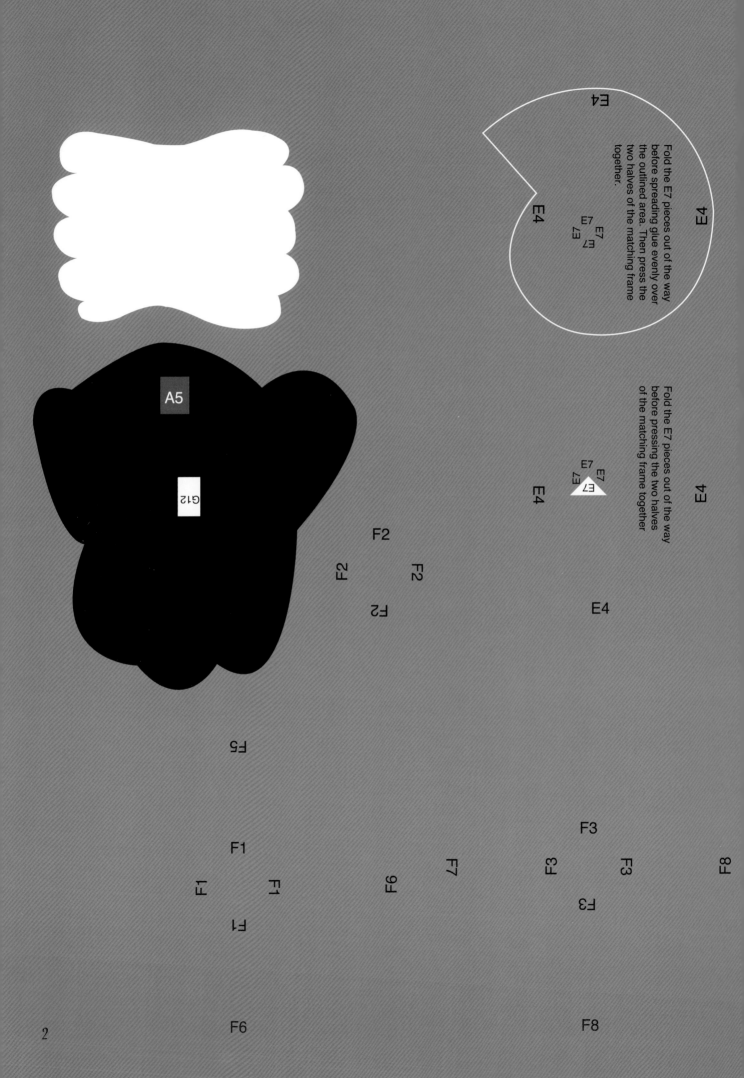

A5

G12

Fold the E7 pieces out of the way
before spreading glue evenly over
the outlined area. Then press the
two halves of the matching frame
together.

E3

E4

E4

E7 E7
E7 E7

E4

Fold the E7 pieces out of the way
before pressing the two halves
of the matching frame together

E3

E4

E7 E7
E7 E7

E4

E4

F2

F2

F2

F3

F3

F3

F3

F8

F5

F7

F7

F1

F1

F1

F1

F8

F6

F6

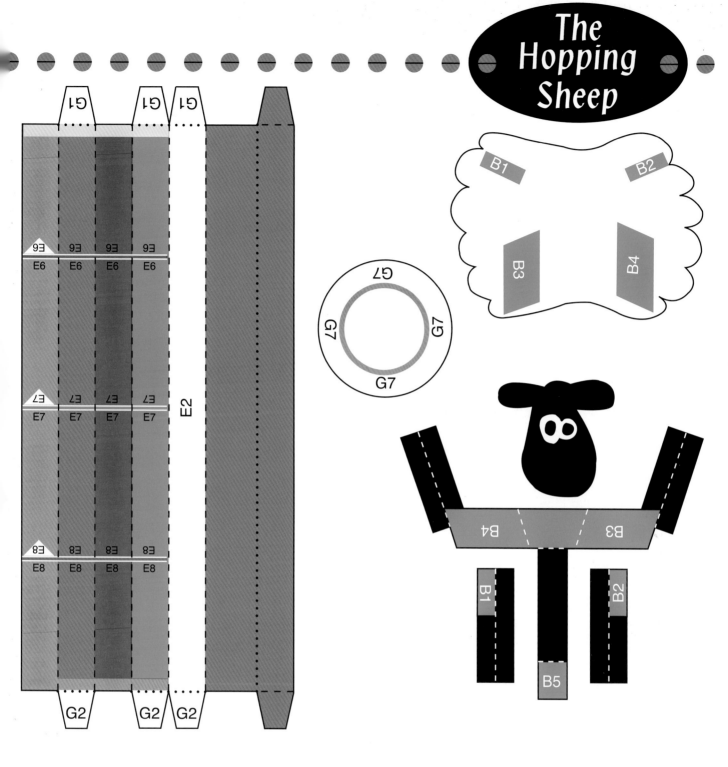

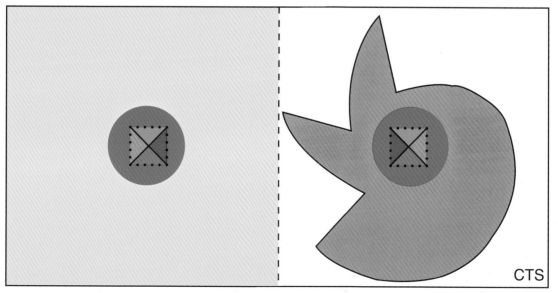

CTS

3

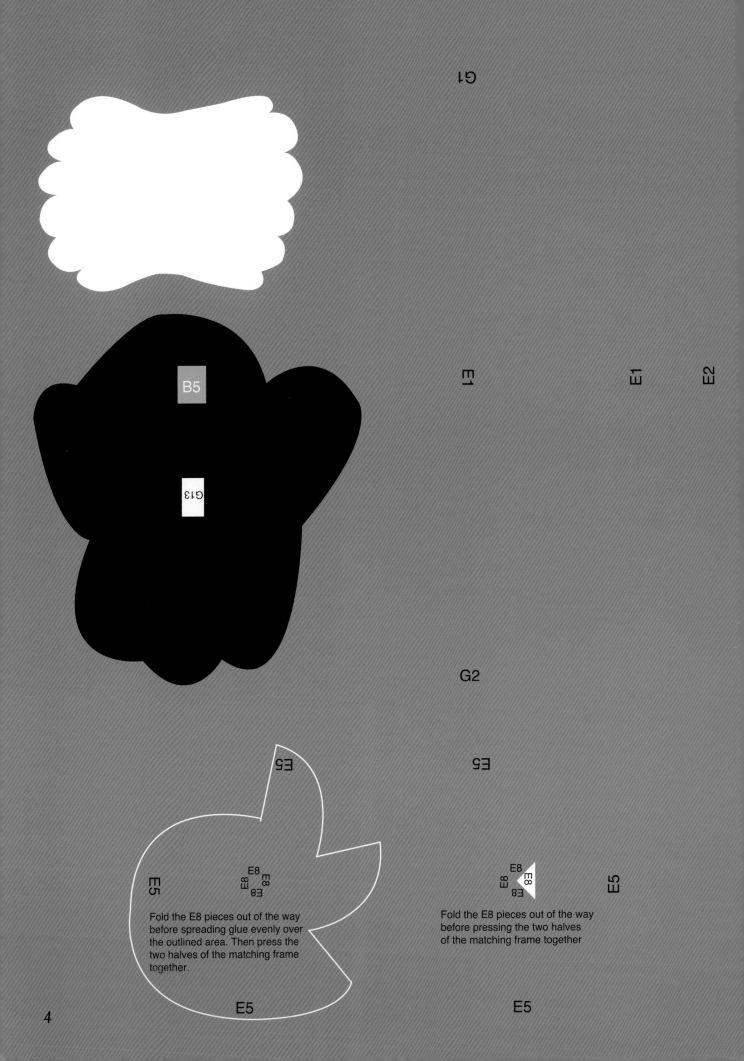

G1

E1

E1

E2

B5

G13

G2

E5

E5

E5

E8
E8
E8
E8

E8
E8
E8

Fold the E8 pieces out of the way
before spreading glue evenly over
the outlined area. Then press the
two halves of the matching frame
together.

Fold the E8 pieces out of the way
before pressing the two halves
of the matching frame together

E5

E5

E5

E5

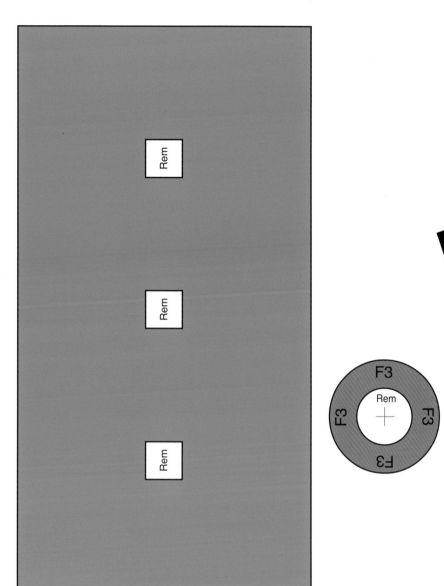

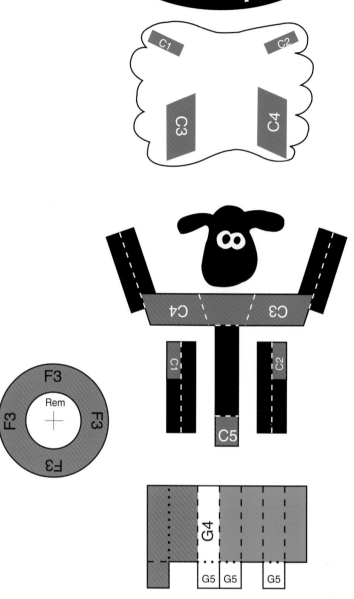

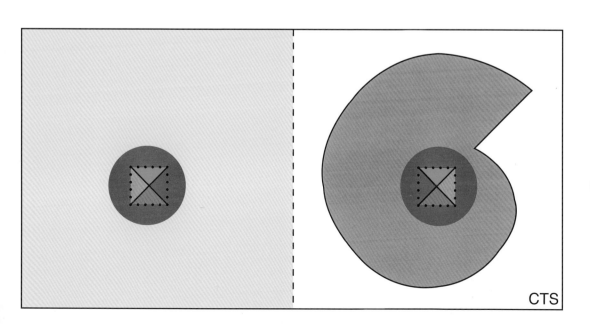

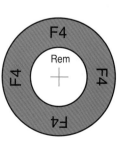

CTS

E3

G11

G11

G11

C5

G14

F4

F4

F4

F4

G4 G3 G3

G5

G10

E3

E3

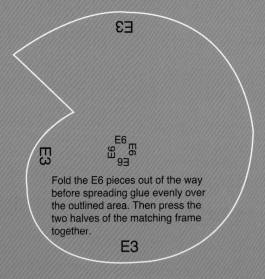

E3

E6
E6
E6
E6

Fold the E6 pieces out of the way
before spreading glue evenly over
the outlined area. Then press the
two halves of the matching frame
together.

E3

E6
E6
E6

E3

Fold the E6 pieces out of the way
before pressing the two halves
of the matching frame together

E3

G11

6

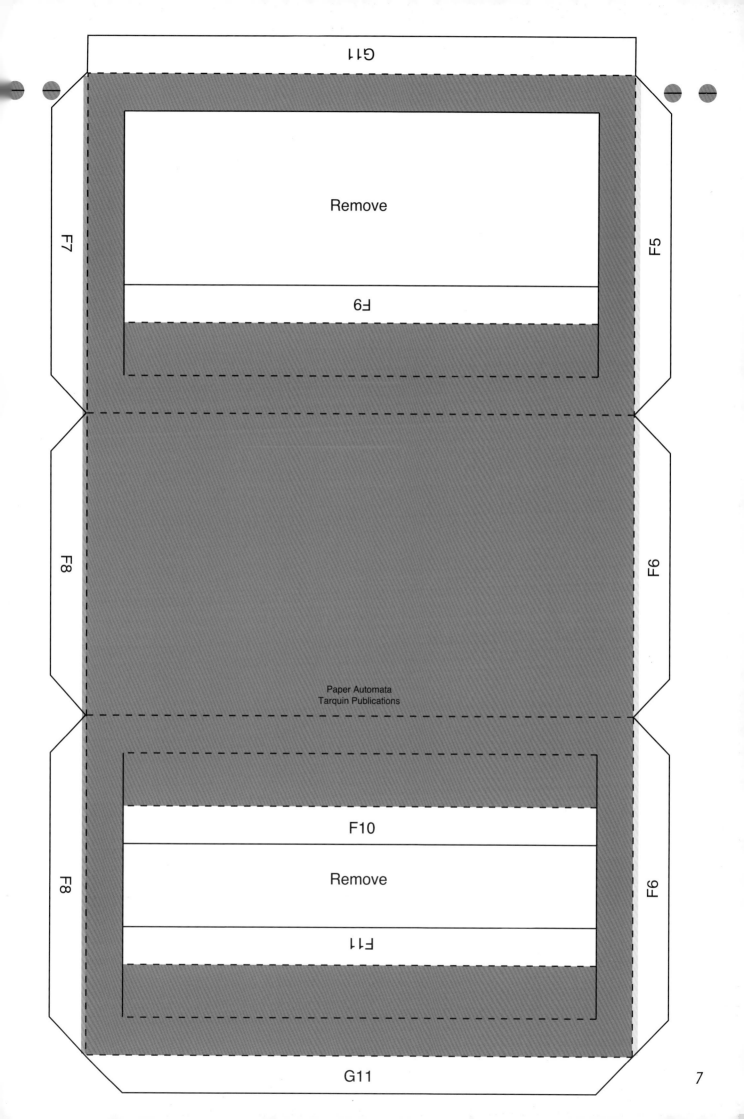

G11

Remove

F7

F5

F9

F8

F6

G11

Paper Automata
Tarquin Publications

F8

F6

F10

Remove

F11

G11

G11

7

G9

G8

F11

F9

F10

G9

G8

F11

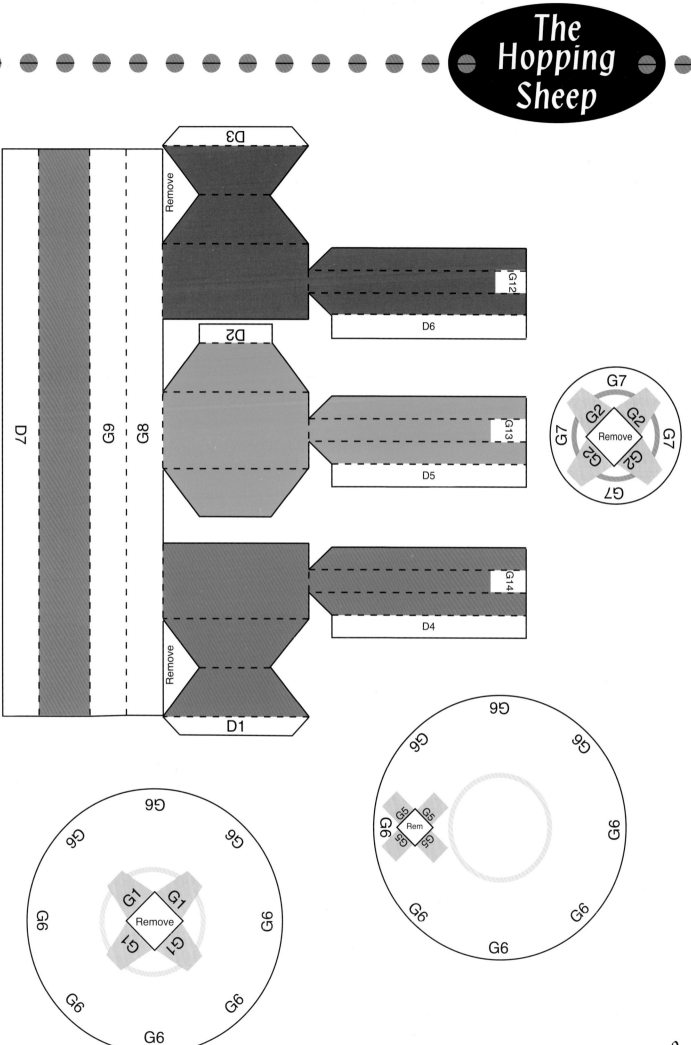

D6

D3

D5

D7

D2

D4 D1

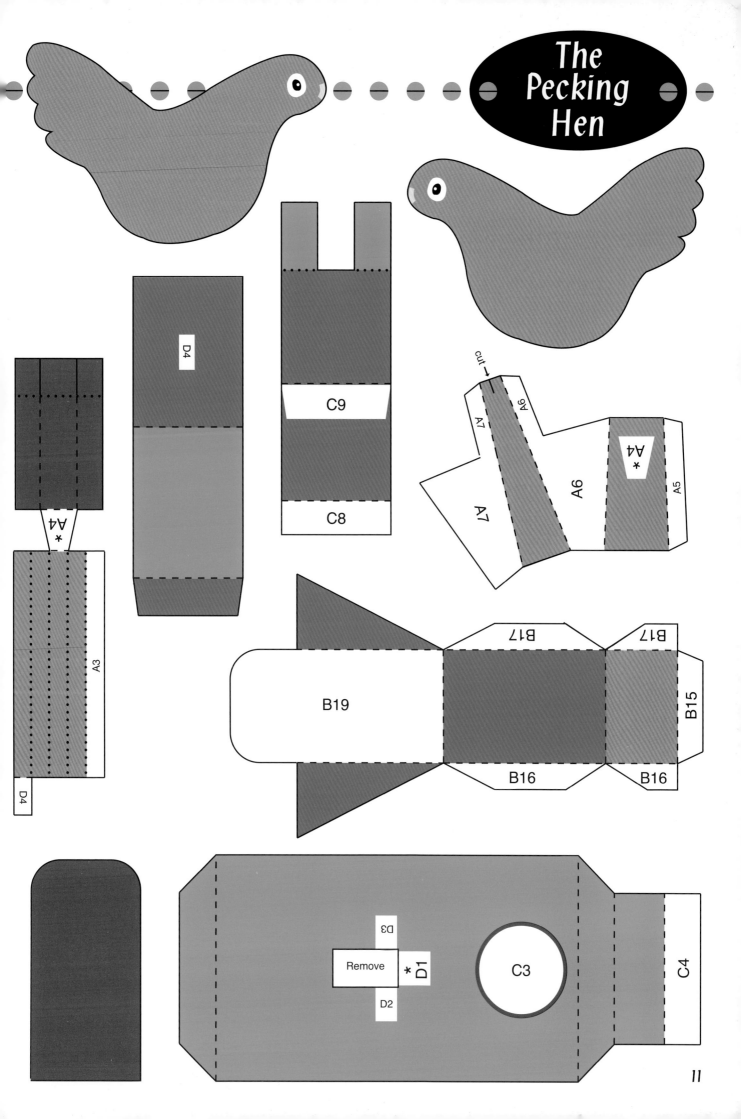

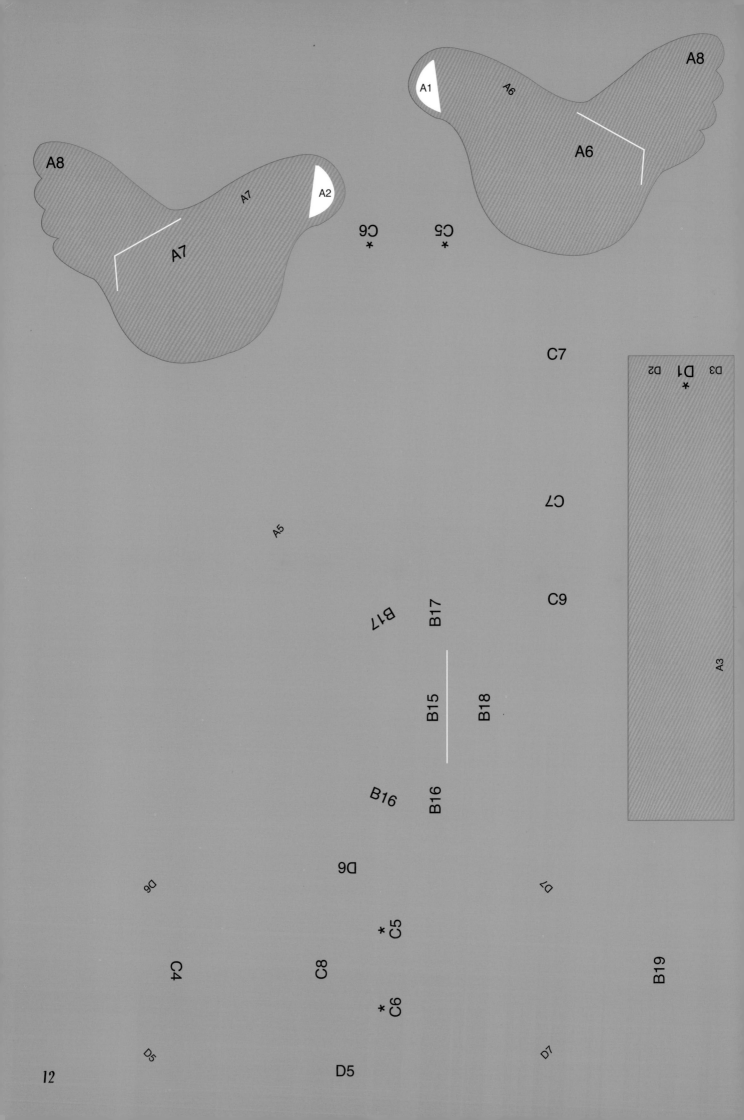

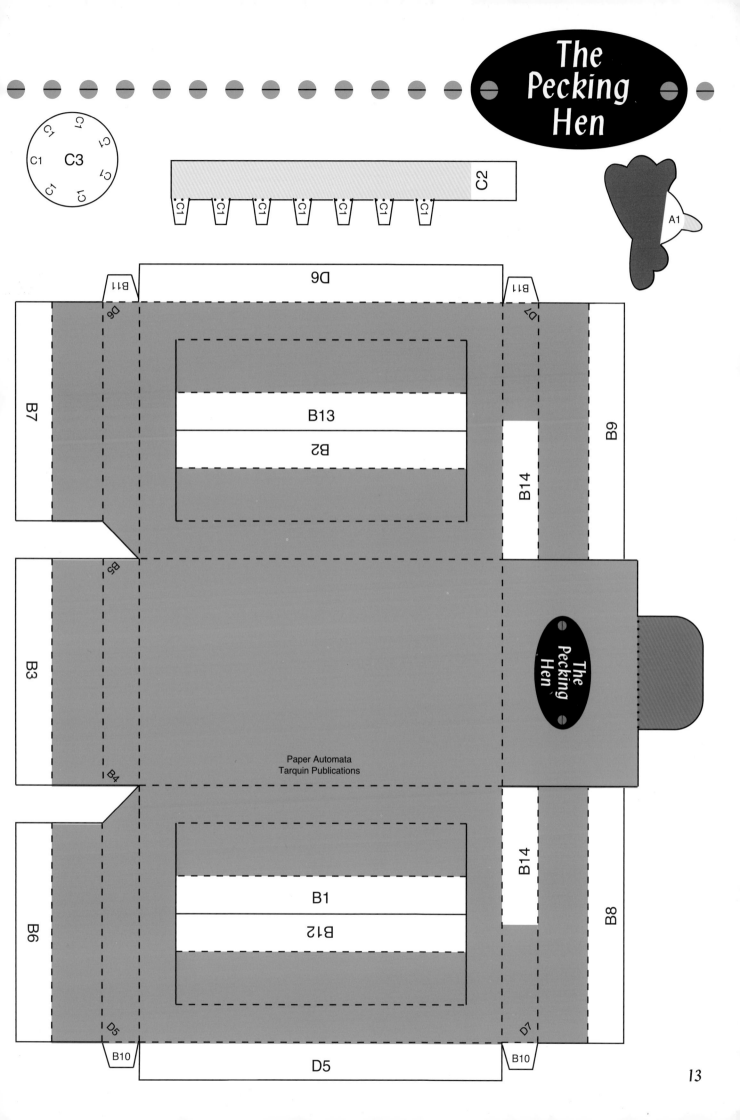

The
Pecking
Hen

C3

C2

C1 C1 C1 C1 C1 C1 C1

A1

D6

B11 B11

D6 D7

B13

B2

B14

B7 B9

B5

The
Pecking
Hen

B3

Paper Automata
Tarquin Publications

B4

D5 D7

B14

B1

B12

B6 B8

B10 B10

D5

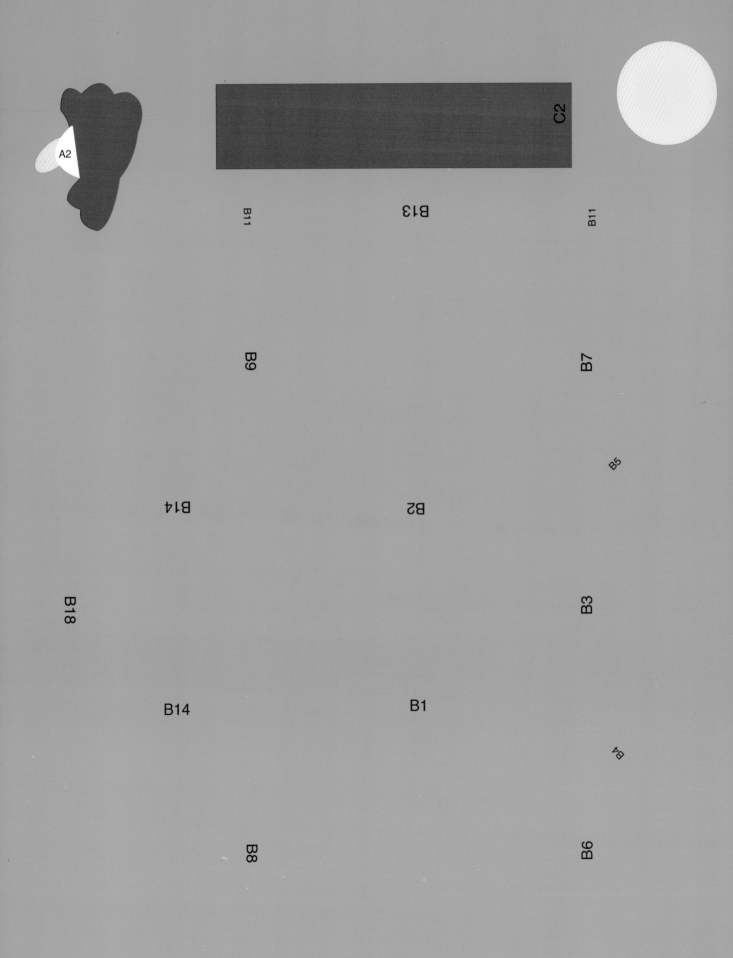

How to Make The Hopping Sheep

This automaton is made from six units and six other pieces which link the units together. Start by cutting, scoring and folding all the pieces as explained inside the front cover.

UNITS A,B,C — The Three Sheep

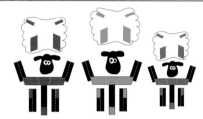

First identify these 15 pieces.

Roll each fleece gently around your finger to mould it into a good back shape.

Start with the red sheep by glueing tabs A1 - A5 in order.
A1: Back Right leg.   A4: Front Left leg.
A2: Back Left leg.   A5: Head.
A3: Front Right leg.

Follow the same procedure to make the green and blue sheep.

UNIT D — The Tappet Bar

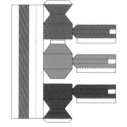

Then glue tabs D1 - D7 in order.
D1: Blue tappet.
D2: Green tappet.
D3: Red tappet.
D4: Blue peg.
D5: Green peg.
D6: Red peg.
D7: Join top strut.

First identify this piece.

UNIT E — The Cam Shaft

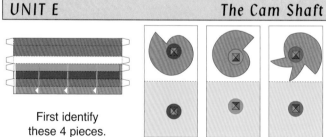

First identify these 4 pieces.

Then glue tabs E1 - E8 in order.
E1, E2: Cam shaft.   **E6: Red cam in position.
*E3: Red matching frame.   **E7: Green cam in position.
*E4: Green matching frame.   **E8: Blue cam in position.
*E5: Blue matching frame.

Special Notes

*Fold the small triangles back out of the way and check that the central squares line up before spreading glue on E3, E4 and E5. Then cut out the cams looking at the side marked CTS meaning 'Cut This Side'.

**As you glue E6, E7 and E8, check that the white triangles line up and that each coloured triangle glues to its own colour on the central shaft. This ensures that the yellow sides of the cams lie towards the yellow end of the shaft and the orange sides lie towards the orange end of the shaft.

UNIT F — The Frame

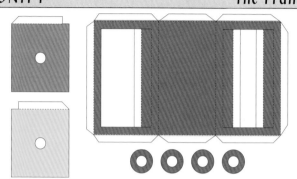

First identify these 7 pieces.

Then glue tabs F1 - F11 in order.
*F1 - F4: Reinforcing rings.   F9, F10: Bottom struts.
F5, F6: Yellow side.   F11: Top strut.
F7, F8: Orange side.

*Special Note
When the reinforcing rings are placed in position, run your finger round and round the circular cut edges to ensure that the holes line up and are as circular and clean as possible.

STAGE G — Assembling the Automaton

Now identify these 6 pieces ...

... and the six completed units.

Place the cam shaft into position within the frame so that the yellow end of the shaft passes through the yellow side of the frame and the orange end passes through the orange side.

Then glue tabs G1 - G14 in order.
G1: Yellow end tabs through   G8, G9: Tappet bar to frame.
and to the large circle.   G10, G11: Top to frame after
G2: Orange end tabs through   pushing tappets through holes.
and to the small circle.   G12: Red sheep on red tappet.
G3, G4: Handle.   G13: Green sheep on green.
G5, G6: Handle to large circle.   G14: Blue sheep on blue.
G7: Cover to small circle.

During final assembly, check that glue does not seep where it is not wanted and that the shaft is able to turn freely.

15

This automaton is made from three units.
Start by cutting, scoring and folding all the pieces as explained inside the front cover.

UNIT A   The Hen

First identify these 5 pieces.

Then glue tabs A1 - A8 in order.
A1, A2: Beak and comb, noticing that the small yellow areas on the head show where to position the beak.
A3: Make the supporting post.
A4: Attach the feet and supporting post to the body.
A5: Body.
A6, A7: Sides to body. Push the slit around the comb.
A8: Tail.

STAGE D   Assembling the Automaton

Here are the three completed units.

First push the support post down through the hole before glueing tabs D4 - D7 in order.
D1 - D3: Feet to the frame top.
D4: Attach the support post to the second lever.
D5 - D7: Add the frame top.

UNIT B   The Frame and the First Lever

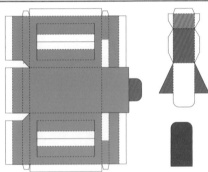

First identify these 3 pieces.

Then glue tabs B1 - B19 in order.
B1 - B3: Bottom strengtheners.
B4 - B9: Side strengtheners.
B10 - B13: Top strengtheners.
B14: Side.
B15 - B17: First lever.
B18: First lever to frame. (The triangular wedge is inside.)
B19: Add strengthener to the first lever.

UNIT C   The Frame Top

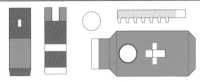

First identify these 5 pieces.

Then glue tabs C1 - C9 in order.
C1 - C3: Feeder. It is yellow inside and red outside.
C4: Strengthening strut.
C5, C6: Second lever support to the frame top.
C7: Second lever back to back.
C8: Second lever support to the underside.
C9: Second lever to support.

16

This automaton is made from three units and an additional piece to complete it.
Start by cutting, scoring and folding all the pieces as explained inside the front cover.

UNIT A — The Head and Back

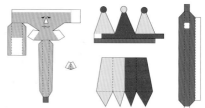

First identify these 5 pieces.

Then glue tabs A1 - A11 in order.
A1, A2: Nose.
A3, A4: Chin. Ease it into shape.
A5: Head. Curl it round your finger.
A6: Hat. Fold the blue band upwards before curling.
A7: Ease the head into the hat.
A8: Back strut.
A9: Neck to top of the back.
A10: Back strut to bottom of the back.
A11: Chin strut to the back strut.

UNIT B — The Legs and Arms

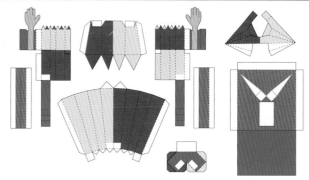

First identify these 9 pieces.

Then glue tabs B1 - B29 in order taking special care to match the ▲s wherever they occur.
B1, B2: Legs to central line.
B3, B4: Close bottoms of both legs.
B5, B6: Both feet to base.
B7: Legs to base.
B8, B9: Complete shoes.
B10 - B12: Close the top of the legs.
B13 - B16: Platform strengtheners.
B17 - B24: Arms. Look carefully for cut and fold lines.
B25, B26: Arms to front.
B27: Front to top of legs.
B28, B29: Shoulders to top of legs.

UNIT C — The Frame and Rocker

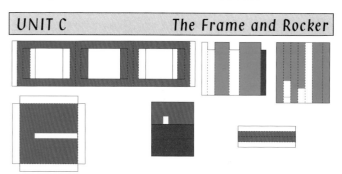

First identify these 6 pieces.

Then glue tabs C1 to C17 in order taking special care to match the ▲s where they occur.
C1, C2: Rocker handle.
C3 - C5: Rocker handle to rocker support.
C6, C7: Rocker to rocker support.
C8: Rocker to base of frame
C9, C10: Strengthener to base of frame.
C11 - C14: Vertical supports.
C15 - C17: Sides to the frame, making certain that the handle passes through to the outside.

STAGE D — Assembling the Automaton

Now identify this neckscarf piece ...

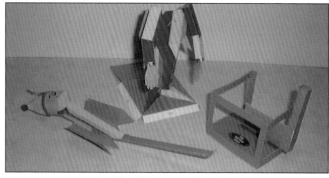

... and the three completed units.

Then glue D1 - D10 in order taking special care to match the ▲s wherever they occur.
D1, D2: Push the back strut down through the hole in the platform before glueing the back and front together.
D3 - D5: Platform to base.
D6: Back support to rocker.
D7: Back of base in position.
D8: Attach neckscarf to back.
*D9, D10: Attach neckscarf to front.

*Special Note
*While glueing the neckscarf into position, gently pull the handle to check that the arms still move freely.

This automaton is made from three units and an additional piece to complete it. Start by cutting, scoring and folding all the pieces as explained inside the front cover.

UNIT A — The Fish on its Supporting Strut

First identify these 11 pieces.

Then glue tabs A1 - A12, matching the ★s wherever they occur.
*A1 - A4: Main body sections.   A10: Make the strut.
A5, A6: Wings.   A11: Close end of strut.
A7, A8: Eyes.   A12: Strut to the underside.
A9: Tail.

*Special Note
Each of the main body sections lies inside the one before it.

UNIT C — The Cam Shaft and Handle

First identify these 6 pieces.

Then glue tabs C1 to C13 in order.
C1, C2: Centre of cam shaft.   C10: Red end through the hole
C3, C4: Red end of shaft.   and glue to the circle.
C5, C6: Green end of shaft.   C11: Green end through the
C7, C8: Handle.   hole and glue to the circle.
C9: Handle through the hole   C12, C13: Circle covers.
and glue to circle.

UNIT D — The Sleeve and Drivers

First identify these 2 pieces.

Then glue tabs D1 to D4, matching the ★s wherever they occur.
(It is the drivers which give the fish its undulating motion as the sleeve moves up and down the supporting strut.)
D1: The sleeve.   D4: Wing drivers.
D2, D3: Front and back drivers.

UNIT B — The Base Framework

First identify these 6 pieces.

Then glue tabs B1 to B28, matching the ★s wherever they occur.
B1 - B3: Red/yellow pillar.   B16 - B19: Sides of base.
B4 - B6: Green/yellow pillar.   B20, B21: Red roller guide.
B7, B8: Red pillar to base.   B22, B23: Green roller guide.
B9, B10: Green pillar to base.   B24, B25: Roller guides to pillars.
B11 - B13: Front of base.   B26, B27: Blue bar.
B14, B15: Back of base.   B28: Blue bar to pillars.

STAGE E — Assembling the Automaton

Now identify this ring...

...and the four completed units.

First curl the ring around the centre of the cam shaft with the blue side outside and then glue E1. Leave time for it to dry and make sure that it does not stick to the shaft.
Push the supporting strut down through the sleeve matching the red and green sides. (Note that the drivers are at the top, together with the fish itself.) Glue the E2 tabs to the blue ring so that the red and green sides match the red and green sides on the cam shaft.
Now glue E3 - E12 in order.
E3: Driver to front of fish.   E7, E8: Sleeve to blue bar.
E4: Driver to back of fish.   *E9, E10: Roller guides.
E5, E6: Complete head & tail.   E11, E12: Drivers to wings.

*Special Note
Place the cam shaft inside the roller guides so that the red and green sides match. Glue E9 and E10 around it, making sure that the cam shaft still turns as the glue dries.

18

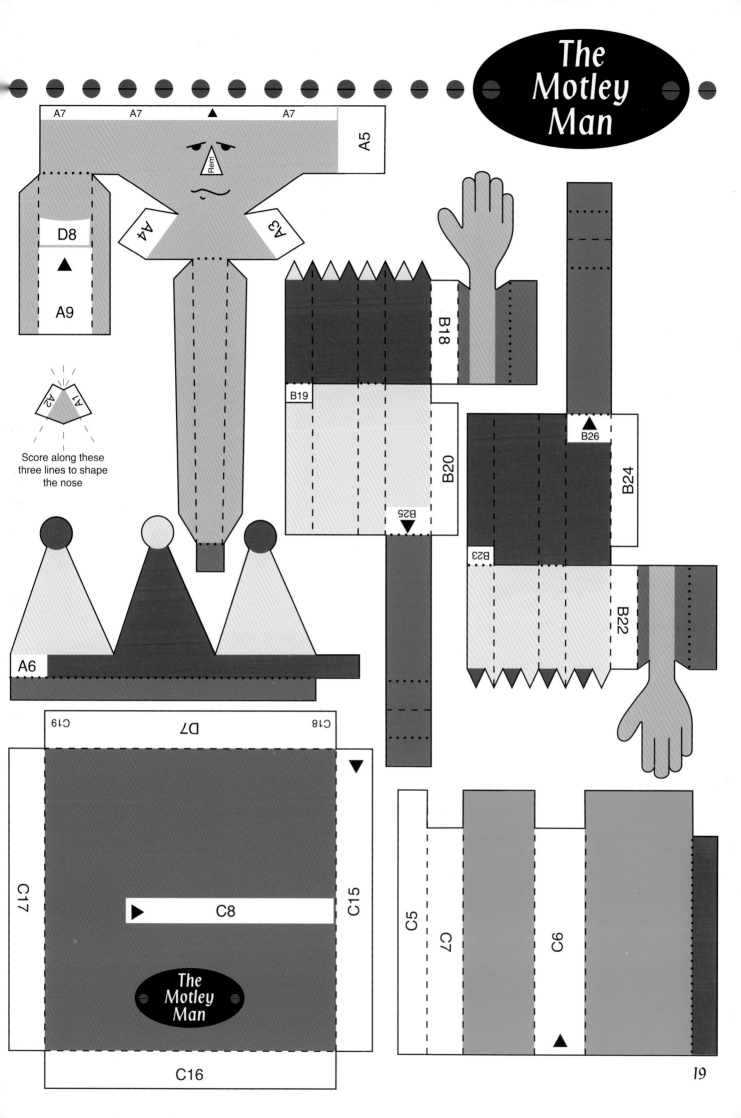

Score along these
three lines to shape
the nose

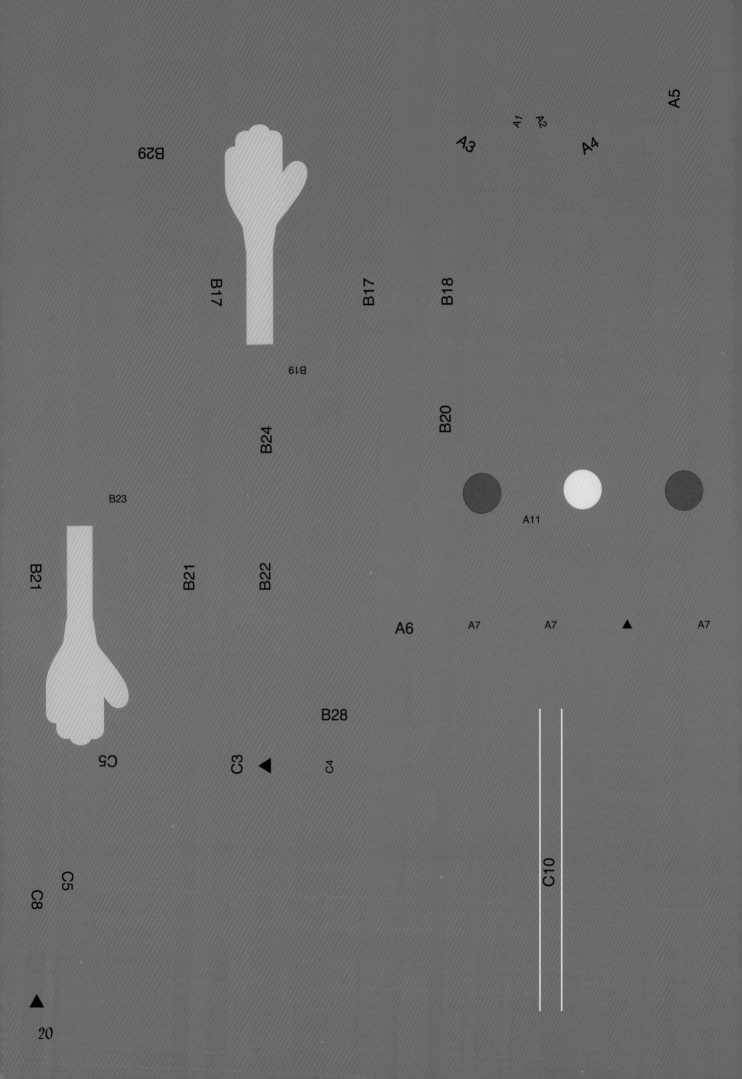

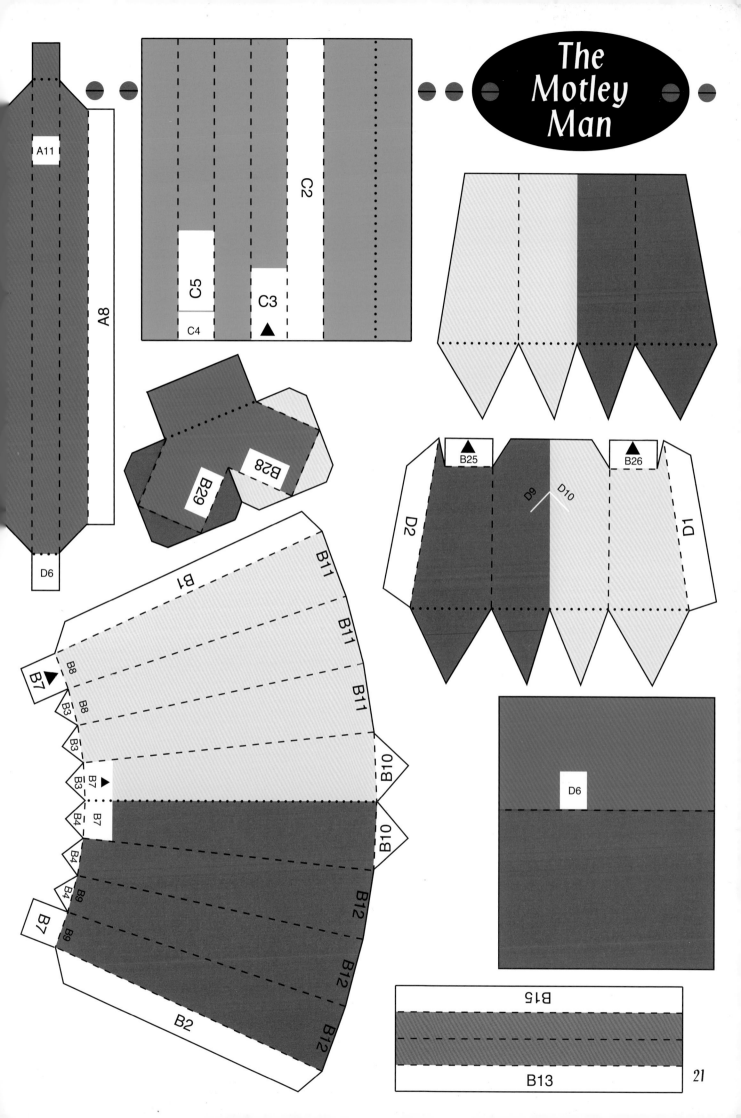

The Motley Man

A11

A8

C2

C5
C4
C3 ▲

D6

B28
B29

B25 ▲
B26 ▲
D9
D10
D2
D1

B1
B11
B11
B11
B8
B7 ▶
B8
B3
B3
B7 ▶
B3
B10
B10
B4
B7
B4
B9
B4
B9
B7
B12
B12
B12
B2

D6

B15
B13

21

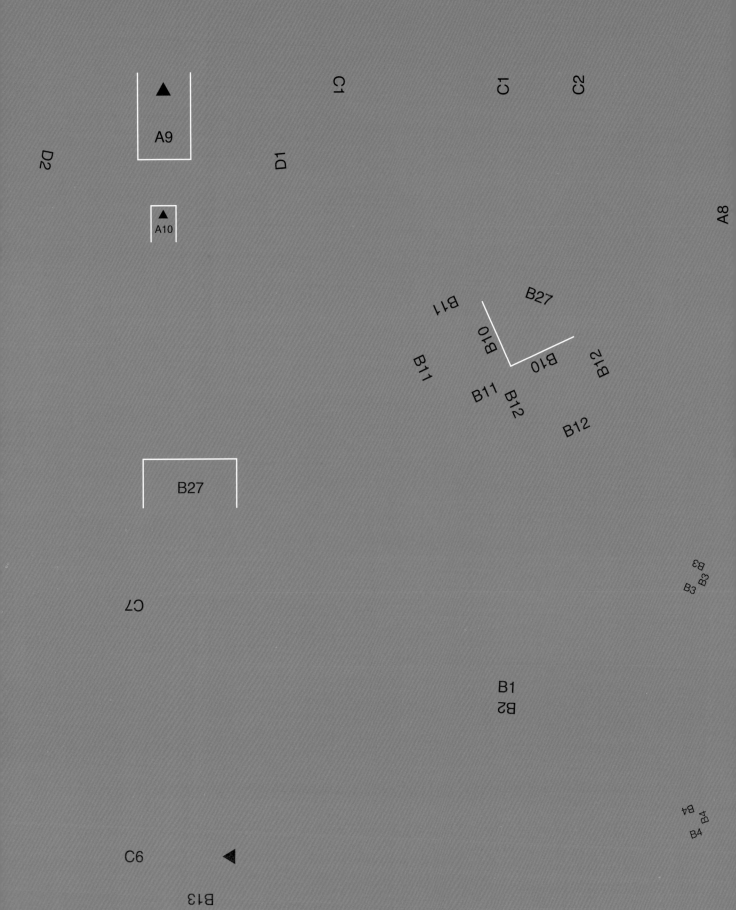

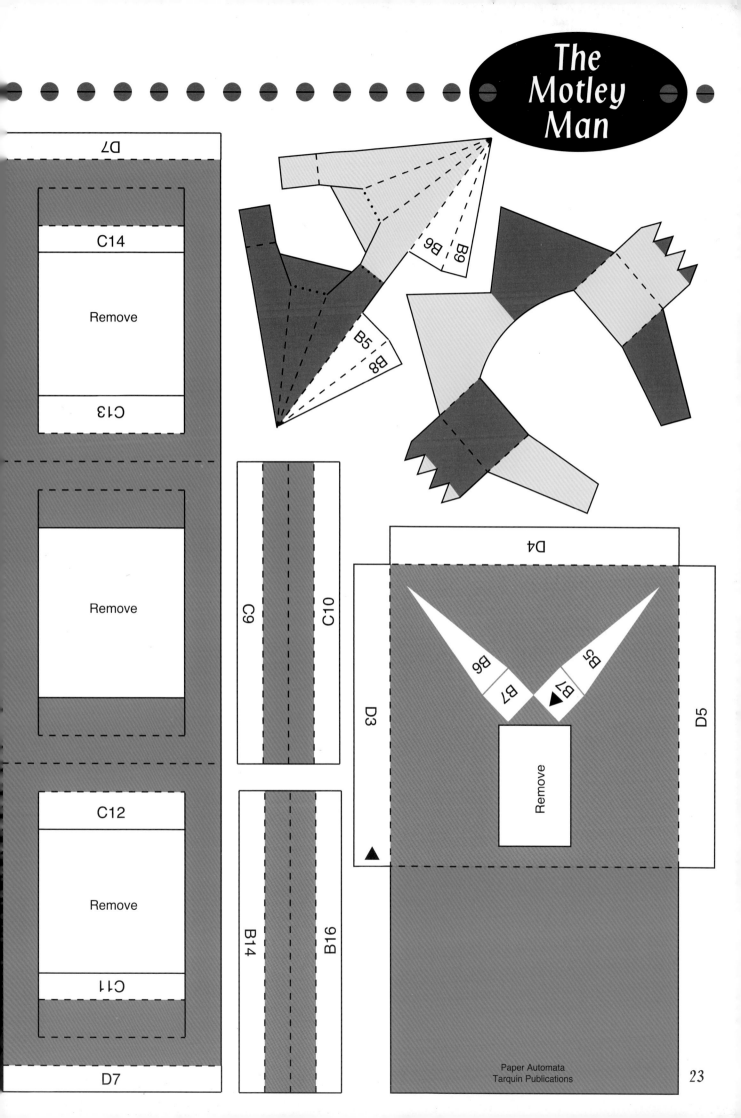

D7

C14

Remove

C13

Remove

C12

Remove

C11

D7

C9

C10

B14

B16

B6

B9

B5

B8

D4

B6

B7

B5

B7

D3

Remove

D5

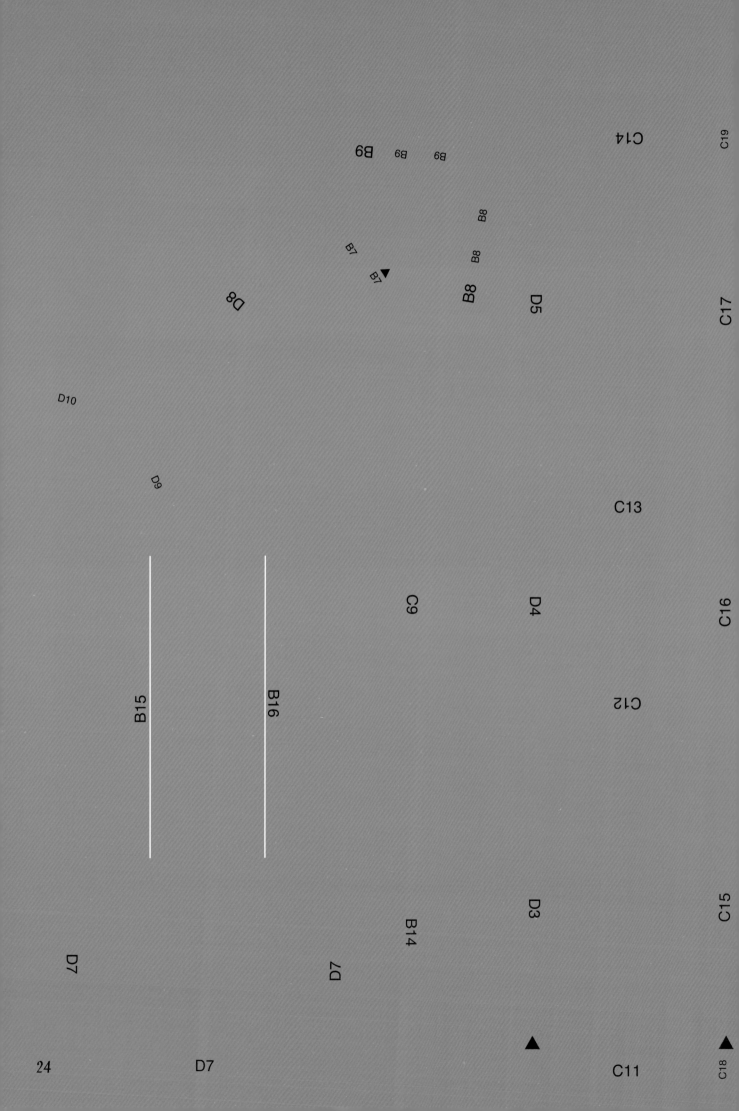

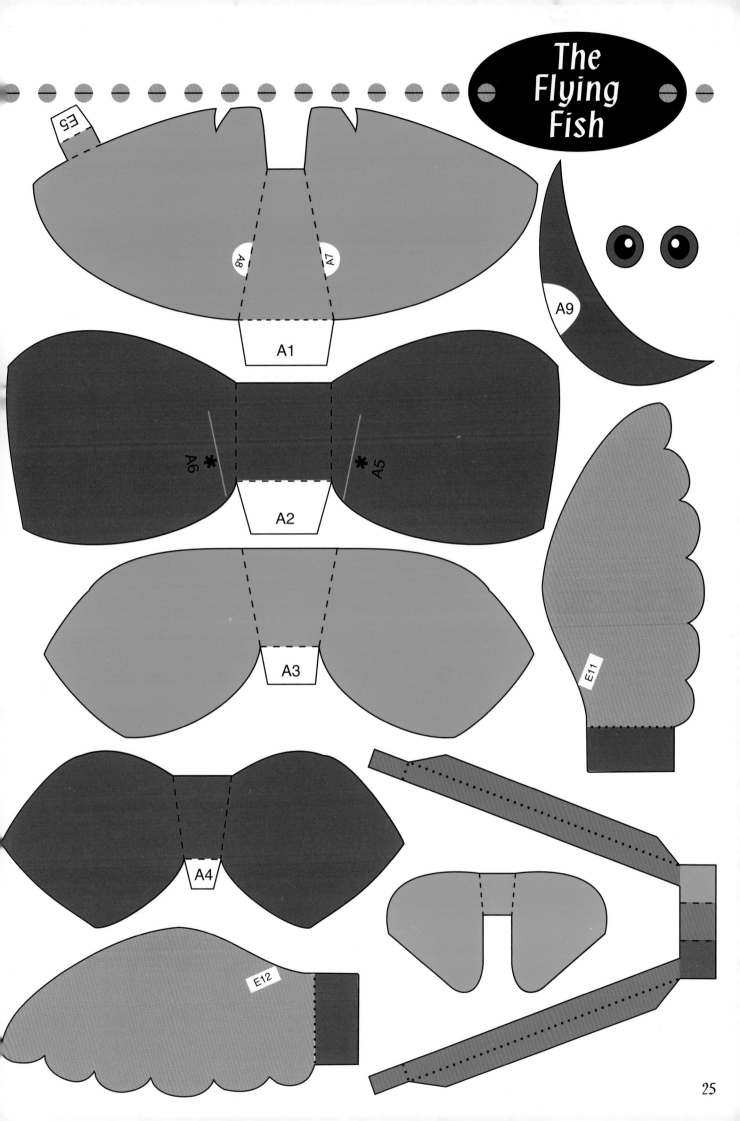

The Flying Fish

E5

A8 A7

A1

A9

A6 * * A5

A2

A3

E11

A4

E12

25

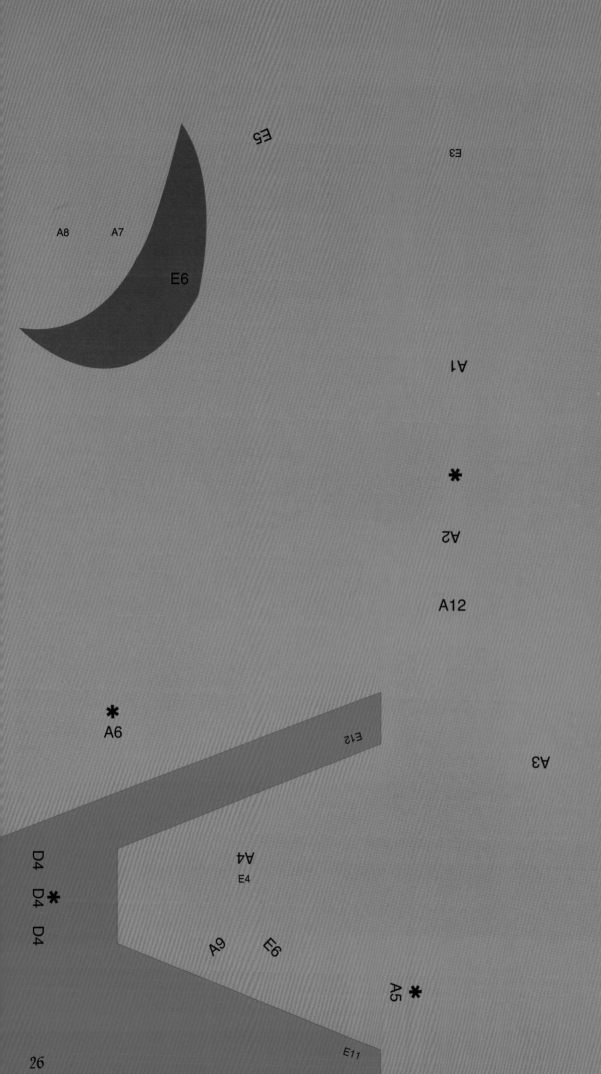

A9

E5

A8　　　A7

E6

A5

E3

A1

A2

A12

A6

E12

A3

D4
D4
D4

A4
E4

A9　　E6

A5

E11

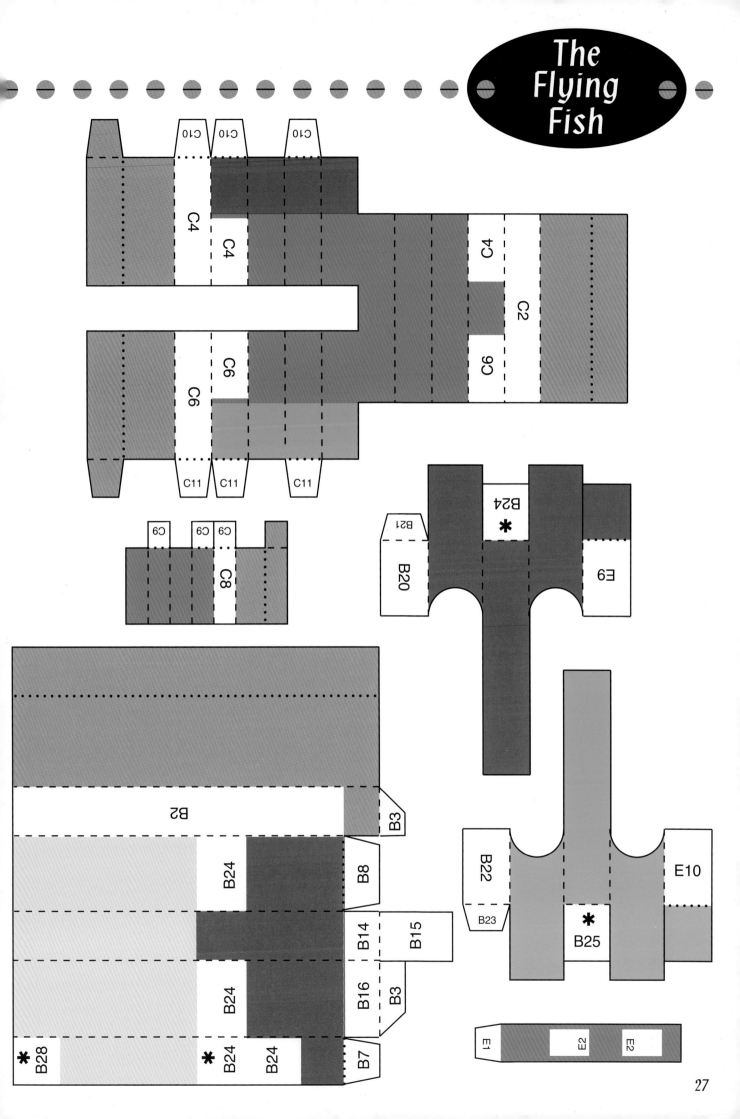

C10

B2

C3

C3

C4

C1

C2

C1

C5

C5

C6

C11

B21

B24

B24

B20

C9

C7

C7

C8

B1

E10

E9

B22

B25

B25

B23

B25

B25

B3

B3

B1

E1 This is the inside of this piece.

B2

28

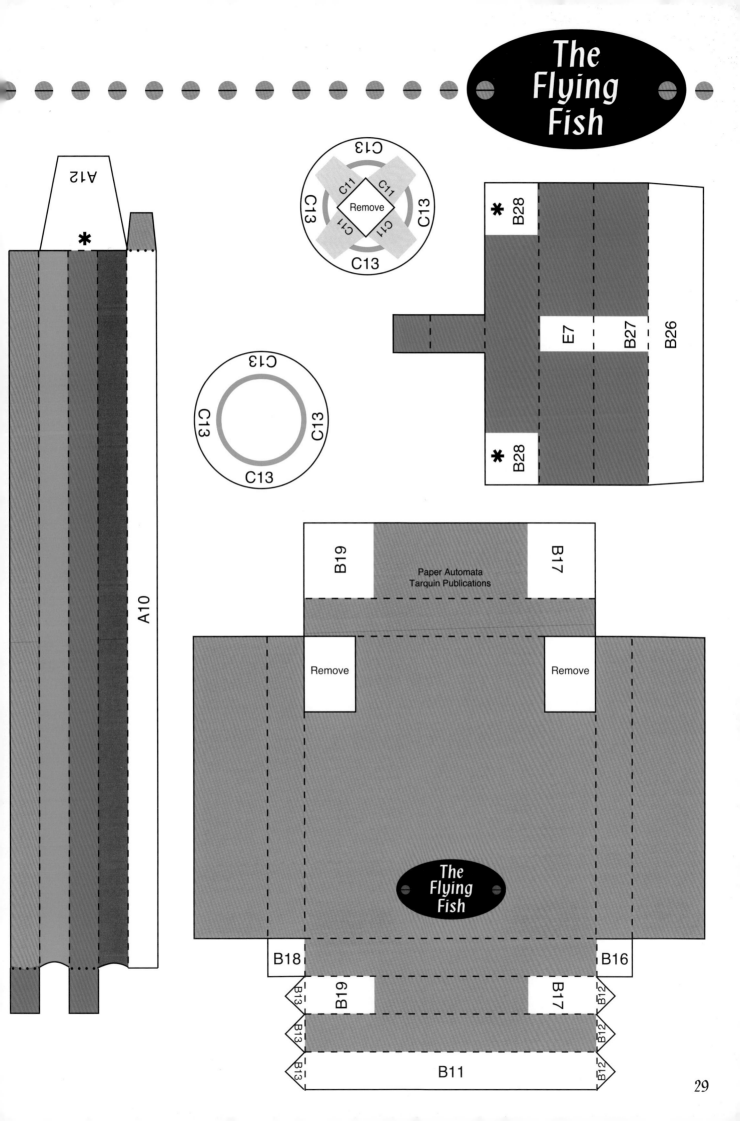

The Flying Fish

A12

A10

C13 C13 C11 C11 Remove C11 C11 C13 C13 C13 C13

C13 C13 C13 C13 C13

B28 E7 B27 B26 B28

B19 B17
Paper Automata
Tarquin Publications
Remove Remove

The Flying Fish

B18 B16
B13 B19 B17 B12
B13 B12
B13 B11 B12

29

A11

A11

B26

B27

E8

B15

B15

A10

B17

B16

B8

B10

B18

B19

B14

B14

B7

B9

B17

B16

B11

B18

B19

B12

B13

B13

B12

B13

B12

E2

E2

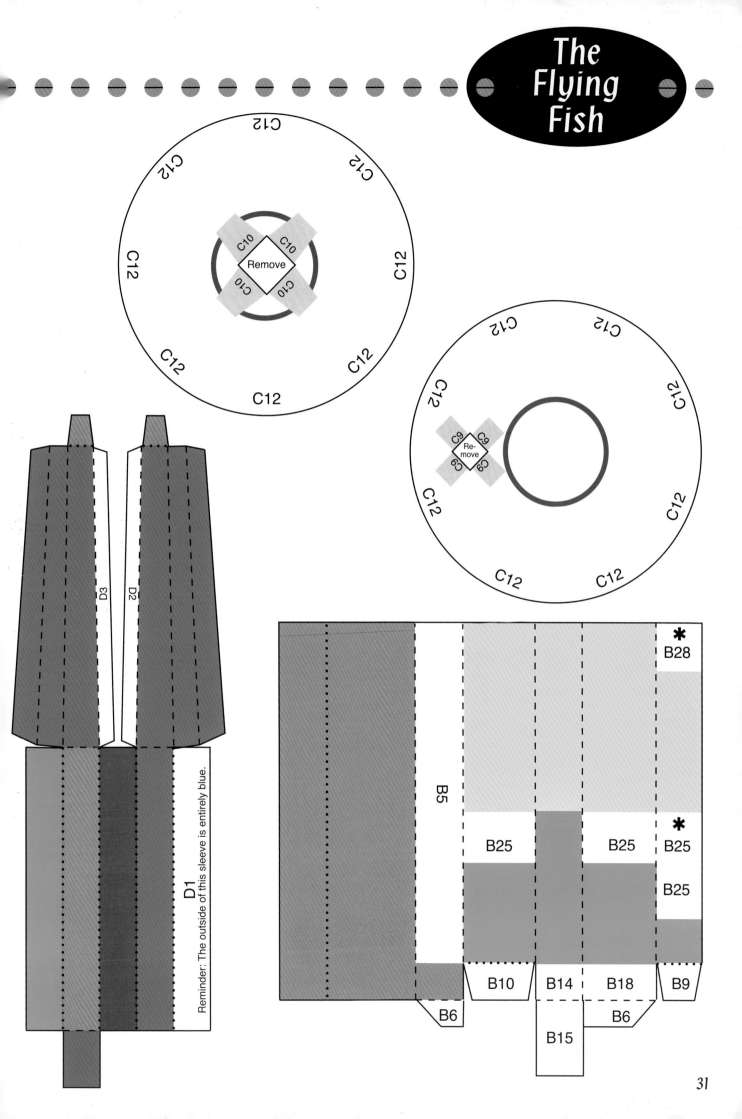

C12
C12
C12
C12
C12
C12
C12
C10
C10
C10
C10
Remove

C12
C12
C12
C12
C12
C12
C9
C9
C9
C9
Re-move

D3
D2
D1
Reminder: The outside of this sleeve is entirely blue.

B5
B28 ✱
B25
B25
B25 ✱
B25
B10
B14
B18
B9
B6
B6
B15

31

E3 E4

D2 D3

B5 B4 B4

D4 D4 * D4

D1

E8

B6

B6 E7